Real Estate Tips & Strategies

Olga Pippy

Prominence Publishing

Olga Pippy can be reached at: opippy@hotmail.com

Published by Prominence Publishing
www.prominencepublishing.com
ISBN: 978-1-988925-24-0

Contents

Dedication

I would like to dedicate this book to my three beautiful children that I am so blessed to have: Krista Pippy, Andrew Pippy, and Kimberley Mattes.

I also dedicate this book to my 6 grandchildren, who I adore.

What People Are Saying About Olga Pippy

"My favourite part of working with Olga was the level of knowledge and expertise she brought to the table. Having confidence in your real estate agent is incredibly important for such a large financial decision.

"I have recommended Olga to anyone I know who is looking to purchase a house with confidence in knowing the level of professionalism and knowledge that she brings with her in every interaction."

–Garrett Martin

"My family has been dealing with Olga for over fifteen years in both residential and rental properties. She found me my first house in two days and wasn't much longer in finding the right house for my daughter. She didn't hesitate to drive over a hundred miles with me to view another property in which I was interested, and subsequently bought. We always had a laugh about 'having vision' for a property and it has proven successful.

"Over the years I have recommended her to friends and she is now everyone's 'go to' agent. She was also very helpful when my daughter decided to become a real estate agent."

–Janice Wells

"We had no concern saying yes to working with Olga. She found us the home of our dreams. Olga was always there to answer any questions we had. She also assisted with selling our home."

–Holly Canning

"Olga Pippy pointed out both the good and the bad whenever I looked at a house. I have recommended Olga to a couple of friends who are considering selling in the near future. I always tell them that Olga is straight forward and honest."

–Deborah Harnett

"I had been wondering if I was going to be able to find a home to suit my needs and my budget. Luckily I had a great agent, Olga Pippy, who gave me great advice and took the time to help me find what I was looking for.

"My favorite part of working with Olga was her kindness and willingness to help me achieve what I wanted. If you want someone professional and willing to put the effort into what you are looking for, then call Olga. She will give that little extra to make sure you get what you need and want."

–Eva Griffin

"Having worked with Olga at the start of her real estate career and now again in what she calls the "twilight" of it. It's a great A to Z for anyone thinking about buying or selling a home or considering real estate as an investment strategy. Learning some "How To's" or avoiding mistakes when buying/selling or mortgage financing are key to successful transactions so your first worthy investment would be the cost of her book."

–Shane Bruce, AMP
President, ACME Consulting Inc.

Foreword

Over the years of dealing with Olga Pippy in successful transactions, we have become friends. I know that Olga is a multi award-winning agent who will work anytime of the day or night for her clients. Only recently, in discussing this Real Estate Guide, did I learn what an amazingly accomplished person she is.

A mother of three and grandmother of six, she is also a certified scuba diver, has a first degree black belt in Tae Kwan Do and has run four times in the Tely 10. She has played ice hockey, ball hockey, soccer and racket ball. When you book an appointment with her, don't be surprised if she shows up on her motorcycle. She is indeed a go-getter.

My first transaction with Olga was almost twenty years ago. I told her what type of property I was looking for and the location. The day the ideal house came on the market. Olga was quick off the mark. The listing never reached the paper; the For Sale sign hadn't even gone up and I already had an offer in.

When Olga called to tell me there was another offer pending (most certainly from someone who also had a good agent working for them) she asked me if I'd be really disappointed if I didn't get this house. I loved the house. The asking price was a good one and within my budget. She pointed out that "dithering around for a few thousand dollars, may mean you'll lose it".

I answered "go in with full asking price" which made me feel like a big real estate player if you don't count the fact that I was standing in an aisle at the Salvation Army Thrift Store at the time. Thanks to Olga, I got the house I had fallen in love with in the exact location I wanted.

My daughter's experience was even better. The house went on the market in the morning. We saw it at 3:30 pm. There were other showings booked. Strategy time; nerve wracking for a young first time buyer. What to offer? My experience came to mind. At 4:30pm my daughter made an offer, good until 7:00 pm the same day to minimize the chance of a bidding war. At 7:30pm her offer was accepted. She bought her first home, thanks in no small part to Olga's advice.

I'd recommend Olga to anyone wanting an honest, hard working and down to earth agent.

–Janice Wells, author, columnist and property owner

Introduction

Do you find yourself not knowing where to start when it comes to buying or selling your home? Is it confusing to look online and be faced with all sorts of conflicting advice everywhere you look?

The "One size fits all" principle does not apply when buying or selling your home. It's important to take the time to think about what you want and be able to communicate with your Realtor. He or she will want to work with you to fulfill your requirements in a timely manner.

In this book, you will learn how to get the most value for your house, as well as how to choose a Realtor. I will provide answers to common questions and an understanding of all the steps from the beginning of your search to closing.

This book is meant to help you feel more confident and educated about the entire real estate process, regardless of whether you are going to buy or sell a home.

To your success,

Olga Pippy

CHAPTER 1

Renting Vs. Buying

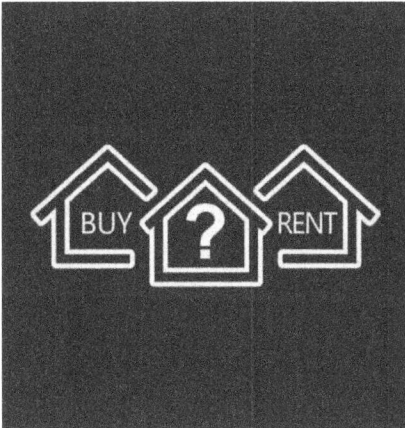

When considering whether to rent or buy a house, weigh the pros and cons to make the right decision for you.

Advantages of Renting

- Renting allows you to move as many times as you want.

- As a tenant, the landlord is responsible for payments, maintenance, repairs and property tax.

- Renting frees up cash to save for a down-payment on a house or invest your money.

- There are no mortgage worries if you do not have a steady income.

- You have protection from decrease in property value.

- Monthly payments may be lower and there are minimal upfront costs.

- You can establish or repair your credit history by renting a property and paying on time.

Disadvantages of Renting

- Monthly payments may increase and there is no guarantee that a lease will be renewed when it expires.

- You cannot make household changes to a rented property without the Landlord's consent.

- You may encounter noise from attached units.

- There is no return on your investment when paying rent.

- Payments never stop when renting.

Advantages of Buying

- You have the freedom to reno-vate/remodel as a property owner.

- Ownership offers long-term benefits of security and homeowner equity.

- You have the option to purchase a regis-tered 2 apartment house to generate in-come from the rental unit.

- Your home can be a retirement nest egg.

- You are able to sell and use the proceeds to downsize or as a stepping stone to a larger house.

- Owning may be a cheaper alternative to renting (due to low interest rates).

- If it's your house, you control the rules (pet friendly).

- Having a mortgage is one of the cheapest forms of loan you can have.

Disadvantages of Buying

- There is a risk of financial loss if home prices drop (only if you sell at a lower price than paid).

- There are ongoing costs with home ownership: mortgage, property tax, maintenance and insurance.

- Mortgage payments will rise if the banks increase the interest rate.

- The upfront cost of buying may eat into your capital or increase your debt.

Summary

The choice that you make is impacted by your lifestyle, stage of life, the local and national housing market, as well as your personal financial status.

Take advantage of available knowledgeable and experts to guide you. Their experience and advice will assist you in your decision making process.

CHAPTER 2

Working With a Realtor

"If you think hiring a pro is expensive,
wait till you hire an amateur."
—Red Adair

Buying or selling a house is a major undertaking that can bring the potential of overwhelming stress. Some people may resist hiring a real estate agent in order to save money, yet there is no upfront cost when enlisting one. The countless benefits of doing so will save you in the long run and increase your chances of selling sooner.

The two most important things to know at the beginning of your real estate journey are: What can you afford and what are your specific needs?

When that ideal dream house appears, it can be all too easy to lose perspective and to begin making emotional decisions. This is when having a Realtor in your corner will really pay off! Your agent has the unbiased perspective to ensure that the deal doesn't backfire and as well as the insight to be mindful of what terms and conditions you would like to present within your offer.

Professional Guidance and the Security of Established Networks

Whether you are buying or selling, a licensed real estate agent has the training, knowledge, and expertise to help create ease with your experience. By taking the time to answer any of your questions and offering insights, you will be able to garner a very clear understanding of what to expect throughout the process.

When looking for a real estate agent there are a number of factors to take into consideration, such as credentials, awards, and the satisfaction of previous clients.

When a real estate agent is accredited by the Canadian Real Estate Association (CREA), they are known as a REALTOR® and must abide by a strict code of ethics. They must be knowledgeable, professional, and personally committed to ongoing education and ethical behaviour at all times.

Studies done by the National Association of Realtors revealed that more than 80% of real estate sales are the result of previous interactions and professional dealings of the agent. Successful Realtors have a broad network of proven reliable resources, thereby saving you time, energy, and potentially freeing you from countless hours of research and sourcing.

Your real estate agent has access to the MLS listings and can set you up automatically to receive a notification for any new listing meeting your requirements as soon as it hits the market. Then, once you are set up and ready to go, you can start house hunting.

Clarity, Marketing and Presentation

An experienced Realtor stays apprised of market trends, building codes and current conditions (such as economic conditions and mortgage/finance conditions). In doing so he/she can provide you with a refined assessment of your particular situation and advise you in preparing your property for sale or preparing you for purchase.

In addition, working with a Realtor gives you the upper hand of devising a skillfully crafted marketing plan. Realtors have the resources, education and training to strategically position your property for the most lucrative sale possible.

Multiple Listing Service and Market Analysis

The Multiple Listing Service, or MLS, in itself is a multifaceted advantage to partnering with a Realtor.

The MLS is an inventoried database of current real estate listings. It includes records of recent sales, conditional sales and expired listings. This index enhances the marketing strategy by broadening the reach of your listing, as well as helping to identify potential buyers. The MLS is also a key tool in generating a Comparable Market Analysis.

A Comparable Market Analysis, or CMA, is an in- depth examination of similar listings within a selected area. The valuable information generated is used to set an appropriate asking price and is an equally important consideration when making or accepting an offer on a listing.

Negotiations and Paperwork

Buying or selling a house is a legal maze of seemingly endless negotiations, paperwork and procedures.

Negotiations don't involve only the asking price. Negotiations includes anything that may arise from a home inspection, appraisal or title search. Real estate agents ensure that all agreements, disclosures, and other documents are completed in a timely manner and are then forwarded to the appropriate party. Their familiarity with the process ensures that no detail goes unnoticed.

At the End of It All

Acquiring, transferring or selling a property is likely the largest financial transaction of a lifetime and involves complex legal documentation and processes. While the do-it-yourself option is available, to list a property independently increases the financial risk within the transaction, and could deteriorate into a legal nightmare.

Harnessing the expertise of an experienced Realtor is a prudent empowered decision. Whatever arises, you will have confidence and peace of mind knowing that a professional brings expertise and wisdom to all aspects of the deal.

"He who represents himself has a fool for a client."

-Abraham Lincoln

CHAPTER 3

For Sale By Owner (FSBO) – Can You Do This Yourself?

"Before you start trying to work out which direction the market is headed, you should be aware that there are markets within markets."

–Paul Clitheroe

The main reason people try to sell their home privately without using a real estate agent is to save money or simply to save paying commission. Placing your home on the market privately means you will have to personally handle the entire transaction. This can often have negative consequences. However rare, there are occasionally times when it makes sense for a homeowner to sell privately. For example, a sale between family members.

Pricing

Sometimes homeowners have difficulty pricing their home correctly because they have a lack of experience and available information. When it comes to selling, it's crucial to price your house appropriately. By listing the house too high, a potential buyer may never consider viewing it because the property may be out of their price range. If the FSBO sets the price too low, they will lose money due to under pricing and selling the property below market price.

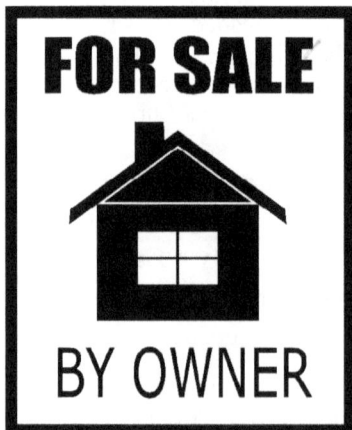

Marketing

Buyers start online and FSBO's are unlikely to get the exposure they need to reach potential buyers since only Realtors can showcase their listings on all the legitimate websites like realtor.com, MLS.ca, etc.

Likewise, recent statistics show that 80% of buyers use a licensed Realtor. Therefore FSBO's can miss the majority of "demand."

Pre-qualified buyers

It is very important to know if a buyer is pre-qualified. This means that they have received pre-approval from their lender for a certain dollar amount, so that if they make an offer and it's accepted, they will be able to get approved for the loan. A Realtor would enquire as to whether or not a buyer is pre-approved, whereas a FSBO might not know if a person has been approved or not.

Time

It can take a great deal of time to show your home. Answering calls, responding to emails, texts or other forms of social media, in addition to dealing with home inspections, viewings, appraisals, etc. is time consuming. Time is money.

Buyers usually want a quick response on their inquiries; otherwise, they will simply move onto the next potential property. If a FSBO has a full time occupation, it's unlikely their work would allow them to answer ongoing daily personal calls, or allow them to take time off work to meet with potential buyers or let the home inspector or appraisers into their home.

Negotiations

It can be uncomfortable when the owner is present during the showing and then to participate in direct negotiations. It's hard to remain impartial and not be emotionally attached to the house and FSBO's can be easily offended with curt comments. Potential buyers may not feel comfortable discussing the property in front of the seller.

CHAPTER 4

What Buyers Need to Know

Q: What do I need to know before I start searching for a home?

A: Before you even start your search, shop around for a lender. You can't begin looking at houses until you know what your budget is going to be.

- Do you have your down payment?

- Are you pre-approved?

- How much can you afford to pay for a house?

- In what area would you like to live in?

- What type of house do you want?

- What assistance should you seek?

Q: How will I know in which neighbourhood I should buy?

A: The right neighbourhood is the one that meets your desired priorities and price. Rural, suburban or urban options offer a variety of advantages and disadvantages. Do you want to be near a school, church, shopping, recreation, subdivision, or on a bus route? Once you determine where you would like to live, take some time to get to know the neighbourhood. Speak to the neighbours before you buy. They might give you some good insight into the neighbourhood that you would not otherwise know.

Q: How will I know what I can afford?

A: To find out if you can afford to purchase a house you should see a mortgage lender. The lender will do a credit check, and review your current assets, income and current debt to determine what you can afford and the amount you are able to borrow.

There are other fees in addition to the price of the home so you need to budget for these. Some of these extra costs include: legal fees, moving costs, closing fees and home inspection.

Q: Should I contact the listing agent to see the home?

A: No. If you find a house online that you would like to view, call your personal Realtor to arrange a showing. The listing agent represents the seller to negotiate the best price for them. You should have the agent representing **you** negotiate the best price on your behalf.

Q: Should I go to Open Houses?

A: Yes, you should go to Open Houses. This may give you some idea of the neighbourhood or layout of the type of house you would like to live in. Inform the hosting agent that you are working with your own personal Realtor.

Q: Is the listed price the final price or can I get a better deal?

A: The listing price is the asking price. Most sellers are generally willing to negotiate. This is why you need to have your own personal Realtor to negotiate on your behalf.

Q: How will I know what school district it is in?

A: Check with the school board district website in your area or ask your Realtor to provide the information.

Q: What if I can't get everything I want?

A: Your only option to get everything you want may be to build a new home. Decide what you can or cannot live without when you purchase. Check with your Realtor for available building lots in your preferred area.

Q: When is the best time to sell a home?

A: It all depends on who you ask. Some say spring is the best time of the year. The flowers and trees are in bloom and everything looks so fresh. If everyone thought the same, the market would be flooded and the buyers would have a lot of inventory to choose from and would therefore be offering less on each property. Others say fall and winter because there is less inventory and that increases the competition. Many houses have been bought and sold during holiday seasons. The bottom line is that anytime is a good time to sell - there is always someone looking to buy.

Q: Can I have an agent represent me on a FSBO home?

A: Many FSBOs are willing to pay the buyer's agent a commission for bringing them a buyer. However, if they are not inclined to do so, your agent may require you to sign an Exclusive Buyer's Brokerage Contract.

CHAPTER 5

What Sellers Need to Know

Q: What do I need to do to prepare my home for sale?

A: Your Realtor will be able to guide you in preparing your home for sale. Every situation is different. Your Realtor may advise you to make necessary repairs to your property as potential buyers will be more receptive to a home that is move in ready. If the potential buyer sees problems that require repairs, they might think there are further deficiencies with the house.

Secondly, your Realtor may advise you to get a pre-home inspection. This is a good way to find out beforehand if your house has any major problems. You may decide to make the repairs

or reduce the asking price to reflect the cost of repairs prior to listing.

Realtors should also advise homeowners to ensure the curb appeal of their home is up to par. Everything should be neat and tidy and your home should show pride of ownership on the outside. Otherwise, potential buyers could drive past and not even be tempted to come in.

Q: What factors will influence how much money I'll get for my home?

A: Sometimes owners overspend on areas that will not get a good return.

It is true that the condition of your home will affect how much you can sell it for. Has it been well maintained over the years? Does it look like a show home or a neglected home?

The energy efficiency of your home will be taken into consideration as well by the prospective buyer.

For some other buyers, whether or not you have been housing animals maybe a determining factor. For people with severe allergies, this can be a deal breaker.

Lastly, the negotiating skills of your Realtor will play a big part in how much money you'll receive for your home.

Q: How will my home be marketed?

A. There are many different ways your home can be marketed. Your agent will likely do several (if not all) of the following:

- Listing on the Multiple Listing Service (MLS)

- Internet (social media, websites, email flyers, database etc.)

- Professional quality photos and/or virtual tour of your home

- Signage
- Print advertising (newspaper, flyers)
- Through other real estate agents
- Agent's open house and public open house

Q: How do I know my belongings will be safe during showings?

A: The seller or their representative should walk through with all the buyers and make sure they are not left alone roaming your house. However, for your own peace of mind, it is recommended that you put all your valuables and personal items away, turn off your computer, and clean off your desk.

Q: Should I be home when there's a showing so I can answer questions?

A: Not unless you are selling your home yourself. If you have an agent, they will be there to represent you and you should not be present. Not only does it make the buyer uncomfortable, you should never be answering questions because you are not a trained professional sales person. You may be emotional in how you are speaking and that will impact negotiations. Your Realtor knows what he or she is doing. Let them do their job.

Q: Should I do a home inspection first or wait until I get an offer?

A: As mentioned previously, a pre-inspection will point out any problems that have to be addressed. This gives the seller the opportunity to repair any deficiencies before the house goes to the market. If you choose not to have a pre-inspection and the buyer's home inspector discovers problems you were not aware of, you can almost be assured the buyer will try to negotiate a lower price.

Q: I have five kids and a dog. Do I really have to clean up before every showing?

A: You only get one chance to make a first impression. Do you want to get the best price? Put yourself in the buyer's shoes. Would you consider buying a house with clutter everywhere, and an excited dog meeting you at the door? Keep your home clean, make the beds and take the kids and the dog out of the house before every showing.

It seems like a lot of work, but it is worth it. Your house will sell faster and likely for more money.

Q: How long will it take to sell my house?

A: How quickly your house sells depends on the market, price, location and condition of your house. It also depends if it is a buyer's market or a seller's market. There are many factors to take into consideration. It could take one month or nine months.

Q: How long do I get to stay in my house after it sells?

A: The closing date is negotiated in the purchase and sale agreement. It usually takes 30 days to close, giving time to complete a home inspection, title searches, survey etc. More time can be negotiated.

Q: Who might I be working with? My agent or someone else?

A: This is a good question to ask your Realtor. I explain to my clients that they will be working directly with me; however, there will be times when I might not be available. If that should happen, then I will be certain that you are looked after by a professional equal to myself. Most Realtors have a trusted colleague that will take care of their clients when they are unable to do so.

Q: How much is my house worth?

A: An experienced Realtor determines the suggested list price based on their knowledge of the area, their marketing skills and by doing a comparable market analysis (CMA). See the next chapter for a detailed explanation of the CMA.

CHAPTER 6

The Comparative Market Analysis

Knowing the value is the first step!

A Comparative Market Analysis (CMA) is a document prepared by a real estate professional to help determine a fair market value of a property before listing or making an offer to purchase. The evaluation of a property is based on similar recently sold, active, pending and expired homes in the same neighbourhood.

A CMA provides the seller or purchaser with a realistic view of where the property should be priced from low, medium, average and high. Though it may be tempting for a seller to list their home at the highest price, keep in mind the key to selling your home is pricing it correctly to ensure that it sells fast and for top dollar. Studies have shown that an overpriced home that remains on the market for a long period of time will end up selling for less than the estimated correct price.

Sold Listings

There are houses that have been listed and sold. They are your best comparable sales because they truly reflect what a purchaser is willing to pay for a comparable home.

Pending Sales

This is an active listing where the seller has received an offer from a purchaser. It has certain conditions attached which the buyer must meet before the sale may be finalized. It is not yet a comparable sale, but it is a good indication of what is possible.

Active Listings

These are listings of houses currently for sale. They are not indicative of the market value because sellers can list their house at whatever price they want. They do not reflect the market value until the house sells.

Expired Listings

These are listings of houses that failed to sell during the term of the listing agreement. It is often because the property is overpriced but can be due to other factors such as price, condition, location, etc.

Your real estate agent has to gather as much information as possible on the property when preparing for a CMA.

Inside the house:

- Number of bedrooms
- Heating (HVAC)
- Fireplace
- Square footage
- Number of bathrooms
- Basement (developed)
- Flooring

- Condo/strata fees
- In-law suite or registered apartment

Other:

- Location
- Bus route
- School district
- Shopping
- View
- Nearby recreation facilities
- Water supply
- Sewer
- Property tax
- Water tax
- Property size
- Exterior
- Style of house
- Driveway
- Land features
- Foundation

- Access (water frontage, right of way, boat access, etc.)
- Garage type
- Features (dishwasher, fridge, stove, deck/patio, pool, etc.)
- Roof
- Rental equipment, etc.

Exterior:

- Windows
- Roof condition
- Siding
- Garage
- Shed
- Patios/Decks
- Fence
- Landscaping
- Chimney
- Recent upgrades, etc.

CHAPTER 7

Step by Step From Offer to Closing

Knowing Your Financing Options

Pre-Approval

Even after a client has been pre-approved for a mortgage, it is wise advice not to incur any further debt, miss any monthly payments, apply for additional credit or change jobs. Pre-approval is a willingness to commit to providing a mortgage, it is not a steadfast guarantee and if your credit score is suddenly impacted you could easily be declined.

You will want to discuss your down payment options with your mortgage professional.

Gather your paperwork in order to apply for pre-approval. By learning your pre-approval amount ahead of time, you are able to shop within your budget, confidently make an offer on a property, and be able to secure a mortgage rate which will hold for up to 90 days.

The following is a general guideline as to the documentation you will need, but additional information may be required depending on your lender:

- Personal identification

- Confirmation of income

- Additional income sources

- Notice of Assessment and recent income tax history

- Statements from your current financial institution

- An inventory of current assets and liabilities

- Confirmation of down payment and ability to cover legal fees and closing costs.

Bank or Mortgage Broker?

It is important to begin by understanding the difference between a mortgage banker and a mortgage broker.

A mortgage banker works for one specific financial institution and is thereby limited by the requirements and current interest rates of said lender.

A mortgage broker is a licensed and regulated professional that acts as an intermediary between a variety of different lenders. They manage the entire application process for you and help you gather the necessary information.

Given the volume of applications they process, as well as the number of lenders they work with, a mortgage broker can generally negotiate a lower interest rate on your behalf. A lower interest rate often translates into a lower monthly payment. However, there are many factors in a mortgage; the interest rate is not the only important one.

Do Your Research: It pays to gather references from friends, family and colleagues. Did they use a mortgage broker and, if so, how satisfied were they with the results? Be sure to confirm that they have actually used the mortgage broker themselves and they aren't offering the referral based on someone else's experience.

Remember, if you have a real estate agent, ask him/her to recommend a couple of mortgage lenders from which you can choose. A distinct advantage of working with a Realtor is access to their tried and trusted networks. While your real estate agency may have an inhouse broker, you are not necessarily obligated to do business with them.

Credit

Assessing and Reviewing Your Credit Score:

Every inquiry that is made regarding your credit shows up on your credit report and begins to reduce your credit strength. If you are working with a mortgage broker, allow them to investigate your credit so that the number of inquiries on your report won't work against you.

Most credit scores range anywhere from 600 - 750. Each lender has their own credit requirements and what they define as strong credit or poor credit. Credit scores generally fall within these ranges:

Excellent credit: 750+

Good Credit: 700 - 749

Fair Credit: 650 - 699

Poor Credit: 600 - 649

Bad Credit: Less than 600

Your credit score determines whether you get an approval and the rate/terms of that approval. It is important to be aware of the factors that can impact your credit score. Don't assume because you pay your bills every month that your score is good.

Taking into consideration:

- Your payment history (including household utilities and cell phones)

- The amount of credit you have available

- How much debt load you carry

- How long you have had credit history

- The number of recent applications or inquiries

Information stays on your credit report for up to seven years. Information relating to personal bankruptcy or an unpaid judgement against you will show on your report for up to ten years or until the statute of limitations has expired, whichever is longer.

Building/Rebuilding Your Credit Score:

The first step is to ensure you remain up to date on all monthly payments to your creditors and household utilities. Being late or missing a single payment can immediately impact your credit score. Credit reports are updated regularly so it is important you keep on top of your contractual obligations.

If there is incorrect information on your credit report, take heart; it has been estimated that approximately one in five North Americans have an error on their credit report. The good news is the erroneous information is quite often removed upon appeal. If an error is present on your credit report the first step is to notify the credit reporting agency in writing. The specific agency will advise you through the rest of the appeal process.

If you are preparing to apply for a mortgage, be mindful not to do any of the following:

- Don't quit or change jobs.

- Don't apply for credit until you are working with a mortgage lender. Applications for new credit can be a red flag to lenders.

- Don't max out or go above your credit limit. You want to keep the credit you have already used at less than thirty percent of your existing available limits.

- Don't be late or skip a payment (including utilities and cell phone payments).

- Don't make any large payments until your mortgage has been completed and you're moved in.

Mortgage Stress Test

A mortgage stress test is new legislation ensuring that consumers are able to stay afloat should interest rates increase. Factors lenders take into consideration with the mortgage stress test are: the purchase price, your pre-existing debt load and disposable income.

Even if you qualify for a mortgage at prime, you still have to qualify at 5.15%[1] or up to 2% greater than prime.

---

[1] 5.15% was the rate available at the time of printing. It can and will vary.

This legislation has been brought in to reduce the number of defaulted mortgages, thereby protecting the consumers, the lenders and the mortgage insurer.

The amount of preparation in order to apply for pre-approval can be overwhelming, especially to first time buyers, but preparing in advance will save you time and energy when you are hoping to present an offer. Further, many Realtors prefer to only show properties to clients that have been pre-approved for a mortgage.

Mortgages

Before diving in to review the various mortgage types it may be helpful to review some of the basic mortgage terminology.

Amortization is the forecasted amount of time for your mortgage to be paid in full.

A term is the set period of time you are committed to a mortgage rate, a particular lender and specific conditions. When the term expires the mortgage will be renegotiated again. Terms are traditionally anywhere between one to ten years.

Mortgage Terms

Short Term

A short term mortgage is generally three years or less and they usually have a lower interest rate than the longer term mortgages. With a short term mortgage you would need to apply for refinancing more often and this could be considered an advantage to some, and a disadvantage to others. If interest rates were at an all time high, you could consider a short term mortgage so it could be refinanced sooner should the interest rate decrease.

Long Term

- Long term mortgages generally have terms from five to ten years. One advantage to a long term mortgage is the stability they provide for easy monthly budgeting. They also allow you the opportunity to maximize an interest rate for an extended period of time.

- Please note that the length of your term will impact the interest rate offered by your lender.

In Canada, the minimum down payment is five percent. When a down payment is less than twenty percent, a mortgage lender will require mortgage default loan insurance through an insurance provider to protect the lender from a defaulted mortgage.

Mortgage Types

Some of the most common types of mortgages are: the fixed rate, variable rate, cash back, and a purchase plus improvement mortgage.

Fixed Rate

A fixed rate mortgage can have a term anywhere from one to ten years with an amortization period of up to twenty-five years. This is based on a down payment of less than twenty percent.

As the name implies the interest rate is fixed for the duration of the term. The benefit of this mortgage is that it provides stable security of knowing that your monthly mortgage payment will not change during the term of the loan.

A disadvantage to a fixed rate mortgage is being locked in. Should rates dramatically reduce you would not benefit from such a change. And should you choose to sell or refinance, there can be significant penalties to do so.

Variable Rate

A variable rate mortgage typically has a three to five year term with a maximum amortization of twenty five years. These figures are based on a down payment of less than twenty percent.

The interest rate for a variable rate mortgage is set according to prime; for example it could be a percentage or two above or below the prime rate. As the prime rate fluctuates, so too will the rate of your mortgage. Depending on the lender, a variable mortgage can have either a fixed or a floating monthly payment. These types of mortgages become far more popular when the prime rate is predicted to drop.

Like any mortgage, the variable has its own pros and cons. Given the shorter term of these mortgages, those that wish to refinance sooner without (or very little) penalty will find this arrangement attractive. Historically, it has been demonstrated that a variable rate mortgage is less expensive over the long run.

A disadvantage to a variable rate mortgage would be when prime suddenly increases, so too will your interest rate, and some find this possibility too big of a gamble. These mortgages can also be more difficult for consumers with a significant amount of debt load to qualify as the lender wants to assure you will be able to maintain payments should the interest rate dramatically spike with an increase.

Cash Back Mortgage

A cash back mortgage allows the borrower to cash in a lump sum based on the property's value upon settling the mortgage. This sum is usually limited to 1-5% of the total mortgage amount.

This mortgage can be appealing to borrowers with a limited amount available for down payment. This mortgage option is only available to those with an exceptional credit rating and those that will be the owner occupier of the property.

Traditionally a cash back mortgage comes with a higher interest rate and will likely have additional stipulations attached by the mortgage lender. Should refinancing become necessary the amount paid out will need to be repaid before any new arrangements can be considered.

Purchase Plus Improvement

A purchase plus improvement mortgage is for a property that requires repairs or renovations. While this option is available through mortgage default insurers, it may not be available with all lending institutions.

Instead of having to apply for a home improvement loan after purchasing the house, you can apply for up to 20% of the property's value (to a maximum of $40k) to be included in the original mortgage. Please note if you are pre-approved for a specific amount this does not mean you qualify for additional credit based on the necessary repairs of the property. If you were pre-approved for $450,000 that would be the total approval amount and any funds for renovations or repairs would need to be within that amount.

A stipulation of this mortgage is that the repairs or renovations must be ones that will increase the property's value. Borrowers cannot include the cost of replacing appliances. In order to qualify, you must have a written estimate from a contractor for renovations before submitting your application. Once approved, the funds for the repairs or renovation are added to your mortgage loan.

It is important to note that these funds are not released until the repairs or renovations have been completed. Quite often consumers rely on their own lines of short term credit to cover the repair costs until completed. Complications will arise if your contractor is not able to fulfill this mandate. When the work is finished, it must be inspected and appraised before the funds are released.

Additional Expenses

It is always prudent to be aware of what additional expenses are part of the process, namely legal fees and property taxes. When a property sells, the previous owner will need to be reimbursed for the current year's property taxes. In addition, a portion of next year's property taxes will need to be paid in advance. Some lenders allow the property taxes to be paid independently, but most have the taxes factored into the mortgage payments.

Offers

Making An Offer

Offers to purchase must conform to local laws and a Realtor will have up to date forms that ensure compliance. Oral offers are not enforceable or considered.

Presenting An Offer

An offer to purchase is a written legal proposal that, if accepted, is legally binding and cannot be changed.

Offers to purchase include the following information:

- Date of the offer
- Seller and buyer's name

- Amount of deposit

- Address of property and full legal description

- Agents of the buyers and sellers (Realtors, brokers, attorneys, etc.)

- Terms and conditions of the compensation of the agents

- Options available to the buyer and the seller should either party default

- Conditions of the sale

- Date of final walk through

- Date of closing

- Key Clauses

It is incredibly important that before making an offer you know with confidence that the necessary funds will be readily available on the closing day of the deal.

Conditions of the Sale:

It is quite typical to have conditions included in an offer to purchase, the following are some of the most common stipulations:

- Pending a favourable home inspection

- Contingent on financing

- Upon approval of attorney
- Conditional on the sale of the buyer's property
- Specifying which appliances, window coverings or fixtures that are to be included within the sale

Key Clauses:

As mentioned earlier, if the seller accepts the offer to purchase, the proposal becomes a binding contract so key clauses are incredibly important. Key clauses are stipulations that may be above and beyond conditional terms outlined in the "Offer to Purchase." While not an escape clause, the provisions outlined can provide security should the terms and conditions not be adequately met.

After The Offer Has Been Presented

After the offer has been presented one of three things will happen: the offer will be accepted, rejected, or countered.

Offer Accepted:

When the buyer and the seller both agree to all the terms and conditions and they have signed the agreement, the house is then considered "conditionally sold".

If the buyer decides not to go ahead with the sale after all terms and conditions have been met, they may lose their deposit or be sued.

Rejected Offer:

There are a number of reasons why an offer may be rejected. Real estate agents know what price is reasonable and what will potentially insult the vendor. It could be deal breaking conditions, the presented price offered, or perhaps the Seller feels it's too early to accept the offer. When a very carefully considered offer has been flat out rejected, it can be very disappointing. When this happens it can be best to just move on with your search. Inevitably something better is awaiting your attention.

Counter Offer:

If the seller is interested in an offer but does not find it completely satisfactory, they may present a counter offer. This is when the seller replies to the presented offer and initiates negotiations, whether relating to the proposed price or the conditions included. The counter offer will clearly state the terms and conditions that the seller deems acceptable thus giving the buyer the option to accept or reject it.

A counter offer cannot be countered; however, it can be rejected with the option of drafting another offer on the property.

More About the Deposit:

The deposit is the term for the lump sum of money accompanying an offer to purchase; it could be compared to a reservation fee. It is a "good faith" amount of money that demonstrates your level of intention and commitment, reflecting your level of interest and motivation.

The deposit is a fraction of your down payment that is held in trust with the seller's agent during the negotiation of the offer. If the offer is accepted the deposit is generally applied towards the down payment or closing fees.

It is extremely important to be very clear about the points of your contract to ensure your deposit is protected. Only ever make your deposit payable to a reputable third party such as the seller's broker or a title company. Never make it payable directly to the seller and do not authorize release of the deposit until the sale has been completed.

If the sale falls through, your deposit may or may not be refundable, depending on the contract's fine print.

Home Appraisal

Having the home appraised on behalf of the lender is a key part of the mortgage underwriting process. This is the lender ensuring there is adequate collateral to secure the home loan. Once the home is appraised the report is sent directly to the lender.

A home appraisal is different from a home inspection. The appraiser is acting on behalf of the lender to verify the worth of the investment and to ensure collateral on the loan.

Home Inspection

It is not mandatory to have a home inspection however it is highly recommended – even with new homes. A professional, emotionally uninvested, impartial third party can assess the structure of the house and offer insight as to what repairs could be imminent.

The inspector will thoroughly assess the foundation, basement or crawl space, the electrical and plumbing systems, exterior, interior, insulation, air exchange unit, attic, roof and more.

If any major deficiencies come up during the home inspection and the owner refuses to address the deficiencies, the purchaser has the option to address the deficiencies or walk away from the deal.

Title Search

A title search is a report that ensures the house and property are free and clear to be transferred. This search will determine if there are any liens, unpaid property taxes or pending legal action. A house with a lien cannot be transferred until such time as it has been paid by the homeowner.

Underwriting the Mortgage

Once the offer is accepted by both parties, the Purchase and Sale Agreement is sent to the lender for approval. Upon approval, the lender issues a finance letter stating that the buyer has been approved for the mortgage. The finance letter is then sent to the lawyers.

If the lender is unable to provide a finance letter on or before the date stated in the offer, the deal may fall apart. If both parties agree, an extension can be given.

Lawyers

Once the finance letter is received, the buyer hires a lawyer to represent them in the closing. The lawyer will prepare the necessary paperwork such as title search, compliance letters, surveys, and disbursing of funds in the transaction, etc. Before the deal is closed, the buyers will meet with their individual lawyers to review all documents and to sign off on the deal.

Prior To Closing

The buyers must make arrangements for house insurance prior to closing day. This will cause delays if overlooked.

The buyers must also arrange to have the utility bills transferred into their name as well as any lease such as an alarm system, propane tank, hot water boiler, etc.

Final Walk Through:

On the day of closing, the buyer of the home completes a walk through of the house. This final inspection is to determine that the house is vacant and to verify that it is in the same condition as when the offer was accepted.

Should something be amiss during the final walk through, the real estate agent or lawyer will negotiate the issues. However, this may delay closing a few days until the matter is resolved. At this point another walk through will be arranged to ensure compliance.

Should everything then be as agreed upon in the contract, at the end of the final walk through, you will be presented with the keys to your new home!

Client Story

In 2007 I received a call from a 19-year-old man who was looking to purchase his first home. This was his first big investment and he told me of his plans to rent out a couple of rooms to his friends and use the extra money do some renovations. I asked him why he was buying a house at such a young age and he told me he was ready to move out of his parents' house and didn't want to rent and pay off someone else's mortgage. "Besides," he said, "I have to live somewhere so why not invest in my own house?" After looking at a couple of houses, he purchased one for $64,000. Although it needed a little work, he could move in right away.

Four years later, in 2011, I received a call from the same young man. He was now 23 years old and with a girlfriend. No longer wanting to live with his friends, he decided to sell the house and purchase one with an apartment. True to his word, he had renovated his first house and put it on the market priced at $152,500. The house sold fairly quickly. He took the profit from the sale and purchased a two-apartment house for $215,000. Having a large down payment and renting out an apartment kept his mortgage payments at an affordable rate.

In 2016, he was now married with a growing family, so he decided to sell again. This time, he sold his house for $275,000.

Again, taking the profit from his last sale he purchased another two-apartment house, this time for $350,000 in an upscale neighbourhood. I keep in contact with him and his wife and they assure me *they are quite happy with their new home and have no plans of moving again in the near future.*

Real Estate is an incredible way to build wealth. Even someone with a modest salary can eventually buy their dream home. Making some sacrifices and planning real estate purchases well, certainly paid off for my client. It took time and hard work before he got to a place where he could purchase his dream home, but he did it.

CHAPTER 8

How to Prepare Your Home For Sale

When conversing with real estate agents, you will often find that when they talk to you about buying real estate, they will refer to your purchase as a "home." Yet if you are selling property, they will often refer to it as a "house." There is a reason for this. Buying real estate is often an emotional decision, but when selling real estate, you need to remove emotion from the equation.

You need to think of your house as a marketable commodity. Your goal is to get others to see it as their potential home, not yours. If you do not consciously make this decision, you can inadvertently create a situation where it takes longer to sell your property.

The first step in getting your home ready to sell is to "de-personalize" it.

De-personalizing the House

The reason you want to "de-personalize" your home is because you want buyers to view it as their potential home. When a potential home-buyer sees your family photos hanging on the wall, it puts your own brand on the home and momentarily shatters their illusions about owning the house. Therefore, store family photos, sports trophies, collectible items, knick-knacks, and souvenirs. Put them in containers, and if necessary, rent a storage area for a few months until the house sells.

Do not just put the box in the attic, basement, garage or a closet. Part of preparing a house for sale is to remove clutter, and that is the next step in preparing your house for sale.

Removing Clutter

Even if you don't think it's clutter, it is.

This is the hardest thing for most people to do because they are emotionally attached to everything in the house. After years of living in the same home, clutter collects in such a way that may not be evident to the homeowner. You literally cannot even see it. However, it does affect the way buyers see the home, even if you do not realize it. Clutter collects on shelves, counter tops, drawers, closets, garages, attics, and basements.

Kitchen Clutter

The kitchen is a good place to start removing clutter, because it is an easy place to start. First, get everything off the counters. Everything! Even the toaster. Put the toaster in a cabinet; take it out when you use it, then put it straight back into the cabinet. Find a place where you can store everything in cabinets and drawers. Of course, you may notice that you do not have cabinet space to put everything. Clean them out. The dishes, pots and pans that rarely get used? Put them in a box and put that box in storage, too.

You see, homebuyers will open all your cabinets and drawers, especially in the kitchen. They want to be sure there is enough room for their "stuff." If your kitchen cabinets, pantries, and drawers look jammed full, it sends a negative message to the buyer and does not promote an image of plentiful storage space. The best way to do that is to give it a lived-in look without clutter.

For that reason, if you have a junk drawer, get rid of the junk. If you have a rarely used crockpot, put it in storage. Do this with every cabinet and drawer. Create open space.

If you have a large number of foodstuffs crammed into the shelves or pantry, begin using them – especially canned goods. Canned goods are heavy, and you don't want to be lugging them to a new house, anyway – or paying a mover to do so. Let what you have on the shelves determine your menus and use up as much as you can. Be sure to check the expiry dates and get rid of expired food.

Beneath the sink is very critical, too. Make sure the area beneath the sink is as empty as possible, removing all extra cleaning supplies.

Closet Clutter

Closets are great for accumulating clutter, though you may not think of it as clutter. We are talking about extra clothes and shoes – things you rarely wear but cannot bear to be without. Do without these items for a couple of months by putting them in a box, because these items can make your closets look crammed full.

Sometimes there are shoeboxes full of stuff or other accumulated personal items, too. Umbrellas, 10+ reusable shopping bags, sports gear... all of this needs to be removed.

Fixing up the house's interior

All your sink fixtures should look shiny and new. If this cannot be accomplished by cleaning, replace them if at all possible. Make sure all the hot and cold-water knobs are easy to turn and that the faucets do not leak.

Check to make sure you have good water pressure and that there are no stains on any of the porcelain. Hire a cleaner to go through and clean your home on a one-time basis. Ask your friends or Realtor for a recommendation as you would be amazed at how much cleaning can be done at a reasonable price.

Ceilings, Walls and Painting

Check all the ceilings for water stains. Sometimes old leaks leave stains, even after you have repaired the leak. Of course, if you do have a leak, you will have to get it repaired, whether it is a plumbing problem or if the roof leaks.

You should do the same for walls, looking for not only stains, but also areas where dirt has accumulated, and you just may not have noticed.

Painting can be your best investment when selling your home. It is not a very expensive procedure and often you can do it yourself. Do not choose colours based on your own preferences but based on what would appeal to the widest possible number of buyers. You should almost always choose an off-white colour because white helps your rooms appear bright and spacious.

Flooring

Always check with your Realtor before undertaking any expensive changes to your house. Your Realtor will advise you if it will be beneficial or not.

Repair or replace broken floor tiles, but do not spend a lot of money on anything. Remember, you are not fixing up the place for yourself. You want to move. Your goal is simply to have as few negative impressions upon those who may want to purchase your property.

Windows and Doors

Check all of your windows to make sure they open and close easily. If not, use a liquid silicone spray that often helps. Make sure there are no cracked or broken windowpanes. If there are, replace them before you begin showing your home.

Do the same things with the doors – make sure they open and close properly, without creaking. If they do, a shot of liquid silicone spray on the hinges usually makes the creak go away. Be sure the doorknobs turn easily, and that they are cleaned and polished to look sharp. As buyers go from room to room, they will open each door and you want to do everything necessary to create a positive impression.

Odour Control

For those who smoke, you might want to avoid smoking indoors while trying to sell your home. You could also purchase an ozone spray that helps to remove odours without creating a masking odour.

Pets of all kinds create odours that you may have become used to, but are immediately noticeable to those with more finely tuned olfactory senses. For those with cats, be sure to empty kitty litter boxes daily. There are also products that you can sprinkle in a layer below the kitty litter that helps to control odour. For those with dogs, keep the dog outdoors as much as possible. You might also try sprinkling carpet freshener on the carpet on a periodic basis.

Costs of Repairs

Do not do anything expensive, such as remodelling. If possible, use savings to pay for any repairs and improvements – do not go charging up credit cards or obtaining new loans. Remember that part of selling a house is also preparing to buy your next home. You do not want to do anything that will affect your credit scores or hurt your ability to qualify for your next mortgage.

CHAPTER 9

Staging Your Home

Before a prospective buyer has even visited your home, they are well into their real estate search. For that matter, they've probably viewed many similar houses online.

Essentially your home is going on a job interview or a first date and, as the old adage goes, you only have one chance to make a positive first impression. It is imperative you give your house the time, the energy and the elbow grease to ensure it looks its best and is ready for its big moment.

In the previous chapter, we discussed the basics of how to prepare your home for sale. Going one step further is home staging. While today home staging is an industry unto itself, there are many "do it yourself" things a homeowner can do to help the house shine.

First Impressions: The Entryway

The front foyer is the landing and launching pad for all guests. It should invite people to venture further and explore the rest of the space. Conduct an experiment. Go outside and close the door behind you. When you come back in, what is the first thing your eyes land on?

Put away any shoes or hanging coats and make sure the entrance is free of clutter. You want the floors to be immaculate and any table top surfaces to be clear. Sweep, polish or vacuum your entryway, but before you do... look up. Work overhead first to spare yourself the frustration of doing the floors twice.

Take the time to remove any cobwebs lurking in the corners and be sure to examine your light fixtures. When was the last time the light cover was cleaned? Not only will a collection of flies deter a buyer, but a dusty or dingy light fixture will also reduce the level of light.

Carefully remove the light fixture cover and hand wash it in soapy water. Do not put the light cover in the dishwasher. With a microfibre cloth, carefully dry and polish the cover. Before replacing the light cover be sure to replace any burnt out bulbs.

Wipe down any spills or spots on your walls. If you encounter a stubborn smudge quite often an eraser cleaning product will remove it. Give the light switch panels a good wipe down to make sure they are clean.

Next, give the interior door mat a good shake out and vacuum. Are there any odours trapped in that mat? Consider leaving it outside over-night under cover so it can get some fresh air.

Any windows in the front entryway need to be washed inside and out to maximize the amount of natural light. Be sure to pay attention to grimy window tracks!

Window Track Life Hack

Here is a quick and inexpensive way of cleaning window tracks. All you need is: baking soda, a spray bottle, white vinegar, paper towel, an old toothbrush, a rag and a butter knife.

Sprinkle a little baking soda in the window track, be sure to also apply to the corners, and then gently spray with white vinegar. Let it fizz for a few minutes before using the toothbrush to scrub the residue towards the center of the window track. When all the dirt is loosened, wipe clean with a paper towel. If any muck still remains, cover the butter knife with the dust rag and gently scrape to remove. When finished wipe down again.

Little details may seem inconsequential, but you are demonstrating the level of diligence with which you have maintained your home. Everything will be scrutinized.

Do You Smell That?

As mentioned in the previous chapter, we become acclimatized to our household smells whether that be from a well-worn pair of sneakers, wet towels, pungent cooking odors, cigarette smoke, or household pets. It can't be emphasized enough: foul smells are a huge deterrent to a potential buyer!

Don't try to mask it, address the source! Empty all garbage cans and wash the containers.

Open your windows, clean sink drains, make sure there is no damp laundry waiting in your hamper. Don't forget about wall hangings or curtains that can be washed. Deodorize any carpets by lightly sprinkling baking soda and allow it to sit for thirty minutes before vacuuming.

Since you already have that vacuum out, give your upholstered furniture a quick once over. Give them a good sniff, and if necessary, sprinkle some baking soda on them as well.

Avoid air fresheners, plug ins or other commercial deodorizing products. Chances are you will easily arouse suspicion that you are trying to cover something up. The best smell is a well aired home but if you have any concerns, brew a pot of coffee for the showing.

Less Is More

It can be difficult for a visitor to picture their belongings in an already occupied space. It is important to present a clear and uncluttered space. Bold dark walls deter potential buyers. Neutral colors enable the viewer to imagine their own paintings hanging on the wall, to visualize their favorite chair beneath the window for the perfect reading area.

Remove excess accessories and pare down the number of family photographs. If you have an abundance of furniture or belongings move them to a storage unit. The number of belongings and furniture won't just make a room look smaller, it also conveys the image that the house is not being well maintained.

Rearrange your furniture to create space and open the room up. The goal is to make the room feel more open and create lots of space for foot traffic. An uncluttered space is a more appealing space!

Kitchen

A kitchen is the heart of a home and it can make or break a showing! You want a sparkling clean kitchen that will welcome the viewer and they can imagine gathering with their friends and family there.

I can't emphasize enough the importance of a n extensive cleaning! At the end of this chapter there is a checklist to ensure nothing gets over-looked. Make sure the oven and stove top area has been thoroughly cleaned and wipe down all cabinets and countertops. As mentioned, pro-spective buyers will open the fridge and cabinets or drawers so pay as much attention inside as out. Remember to remove any refrigerator magnets or papers from the fridge.

If you have a garbage disposal, run a couple of pieces of citrus fruit through it to clean any ac-cumulated odor. If there is a dishwasher, place a cup of white vinegar in an empty dishwasher and put it on the hot water setting. This will re-move any grease build up as well as neutralize any odors.

Consider a vase of fresh flowers on the counter. Keep it simple and keep it clean.

Before refacing any cabinets or replacing coun-tertops consult your Realtor for feedback. It is too easy to invest in renovations that may not be recouped. Perhaps a new set of handles or a fresh coat of paint will suffice – trust your Real-tor's judgement and expertise.

Bathrooms

Bathrooms are just as important as the kitchen for increasing the perceived value of the home. Presenting a tranquil spa-like bathroom is sure to entice a buyer.

Clean, clean, clean! Wipe down the ceiling and walls, scrub grout and shower door and make that toilet shine! Bathroom wall grime can be an immediate red flag to potential buyers. In a spray bottle mix one part water and one part bleach, then spray and wipe down all walls. When done, put away all of the cleaning sup-plies, including the plunger and toilet brush.

Clear the bathroom countertops and be sure to remove all personal hygiene products including toothbrushes and other toiletries. Tuck away the bathroom scale and do everything you can to depersonalize this space.

Lay out clean, fresh towels folded in an orderly fashion and consider placing a new rug next to the tub or shower. An unlit candle on the countertop or edge of the bathtub is more than enough. Remember less is more!

As mentioned with kitchen, the same applies to bathroom. Consult your Realtor for feedback before you make any costly upgrades.

Bedrooms

The bedrooms are second only to the bathroom as the most intimate place in your home. Depersonalize this space as much as possible so the viewer doesn't feel like an intruder and can imagine their own belongings in the space.

The bed is the biggest piece of furniture in the bedroom and it is automatically a focal point. It sets the tone. Consider buying a fresh "bed in a bag" that contains a new duvet and matching pillows. It is a quick, simple and impactful fix.

Minor Repairs

Most buyers want to move in without having to do any maintenance so even the smallest repairs can overwhelm a prospective buyer. Make any minor repairs and consult with your agent for further feedback before the first viewing. Consult the handy checklist below to ensure nothing is missed.

I can't emphasize enough how important it is for your property to be shown in its best possible condition. People are always willing to pay premium, so you want to make sure that absolutely every inch of the house has been cleaned thoroughly. Not only will you potentially increase any offers made, but you can also seriously reduce the amount of time your house is on the market.

Homeowner's Checklist:

All Rooms:

- ☐ Remove clutter
- ☐ Empty all wastebaskets
- ☐ Clear all table tops
- ☐ Depersonalize space (put away all clothing and shoes)
- ☐ Dust walls from the top down
- ☐ Wipe down all light switches and electrical outlet plates

- ☐ Wash baseboards

- ☐ Dust all furniture

- ☐ Wash windows inside and out

- ☐ Clean window tracks

- ☐ Launder window furnishings

- ☐ Clean blinds

- ☐ Mop and wax all hardwood floors

- ☐ Have windows open as much as possible to allow fresh air

- ☐ Address animal odors (i.e.: litter box)

Kitchen:

- ☐ Clean inside refrigerator, wipe down and buff exterior

- ☐ Remove all refrigerator magnets, papers or notices

- ☐ Clean inside oven

- ☐ Clean stovetop

- ☐ Degrease surrounding stove area including overhead fan

- ☐ Clean windows inside and out

- ☐ Clean window tracks

- ☐ Process citrus fruit trimmings in garburator

- ☐ Run vinegar through dishwasher

- ☐ Clean sink drains

- ☐ Clean and polish sinks

- ☐ Clean sink backsplash area

- ☐ Clean all grout and tiles

- ☐ Clean all lighting fixtures

- ☐ Wipe down all light switch and electrical outlet plates

- ☐ Clear off countertops except for coffee maker

- ☐ Put away all small appliances

- ☐ Sweep, mop and polish floor

- ☐ Empty and wash all waste bins

- ☐ Consider updating cabinet hardware

Always consult your real estate agent before making any costly upgrades.

Bathroom:

- ☐ Clean and spray all walls

- ☐ Clean windows inside and out

- ☐ Clean window tracks
- ☐ Replace any burnt out lightbulbs
- ☐ Clean light fixtures
- ☐ Clear all countertops
- ☐ Empty wastebaskets
- ☐ Scour shower doors/clean shower curtain
- ☐ Clean mirror
- ☐ Polish fixtures (including toilet paper dispenser)
- ☐ Scrub tub
- ☐ Scrub toilet bowl, wash tank, and clean beneath and all surrounding areas
- ☐ Put away scale
- ☐ Put away all robes and personal items
- ☐ Put away all hygiene products (including toothbrushes)
- ☐ Lay out clean towels
- ☐ Consider new rug by tub or shower

Minor Repair Checklist:

- ☐ Clean ceiling fan

- ☐ Clean fireplace hearth and chimney
- ☐ Replace all burnt out light bulbs
- ☐ Patch holes
- ☐ Touch up paint and trim
- ☐ Lubricate squeaking doors, cabinets or windows
- ☐ Repair or replace any broken window blinds
- ☐ Replace any cracked tiles
- ☐ Repair tile grout

CHAPTER 10

The Importance of Curb Appeal

Curb appeal makes a difference between a house that sells quickly or one that flounders on the market for months. Your home's exterior and yard will either invite or repel potential viewers. It doesn't matter how much effort you've put into preparing the interior, if the exterior doesn't reflect that, your efforts will have been for naught.

In order to maximize property value, you need to focus on attracting buyers from the moment they *first lay eyes* on the home, whether online or in person. Head out onto the street to assess your home and try to envision how it is perceived with the eyes of someone visiting for the first time.

There are a variety of zones to consider when analyzing curb appeal such as: the address, the approach, the yard and perimeter, and the final impact of curb appeal, the portal to the interior experience... the doorway.

Each section below has helpful inexpensive tips to help you receive your asking price or more as quickly as possible. At the end of the chapter there is also a seasonal checklist because, as previously mentioned, homes don't just sell during the sunny months.

The Address

Whether hung streetside or mounted on the building, your house address is a focal point unto itself. It is the very first thing that is being looked for, in essence, it is its identity! As such you want to make sure that the house number is readily seen and is attractive.

An easily evident address isn't just an aesthetic detail, this is a safety measure, because if you can't see the house number, neither can fire-fighters or other first responders.

Visit your local hardware store and browse their selection of larger and more contemporary numbers while keeping your house's style and architecture in mind. You want the address to declare "You are here!" without any room for confusion.

Look Up

Work from the top down so that you don't create more work for yourself; there is no point in cleaning your yard if the roof has yet to be tended to.

If your roof has missing shingles or damage, this needs to be professionally repaired as well as cleared of any moss, weeds or debris. The chimney will also need to be inspected, even if it appears to be in good condition from the outside. Cleaning a chimney is not a do it yourself job and needs to be inspected annually by a chimney sweep even if not used on a regular basis.

All gutters need to be cleaned and any loose gutters reattached, ensuring that all downspouts are clear and flowing with ease. A blocked gutter will damage the roof and any overflow will pool next to the foundation, eventually ending up in the basement or crawlspace.

All of the above will be keen areas of interest for home inspectors, so do the preliminary work now in order to start your sale on the right foot. Reducing complications will likely shorten the number of cautions on the home inspection report thereby impressing your prospective buyer.

The Approach

For the sake of this chapter, I refer to "the approach" as the driveway and any path that leads to your home.

Remove any vegetation that may be popping up through cracks or walkway seams. Sweep and pressure wash the driveway and any sidewalk areas leading to your home.

Pressure washing is an incredibly cost-effective way of instantly sprucing up your home's appearance by removing moss, mold or mildew. Be sure to read the operator's manual to avoid accidents or injury. Wear protective eyewear and dress for the possibility of getting drenched! In addition, take precautions to protect areas vulnerable to spray.

For stains on your driveway there are many effective commercial degreasers on the market. They can help remove the stain prior to pressure washing the driveway.

Before you put away the pressure washer, remember to go around to the backyard and tend to any paths, brick walls, and patio areas including patio furnishings if need be.

The Garage

The garage door is a large blank canvas and it's important that it be as well maintained as the front door. Don't get overwhelmed, you don't have to replace it! A simple garage door makeover can be relatively inexpensive yet make a world of difference. A fresh coat of paint and updated hardware may suffice. You may also purchase garage door window decals to instantly transform any bland garage door.

The interior of the garage is just as important. Be sure to keep the garage floor well swept and clean. The same degreasers suggested for your driveway would likely work for any stains on the garage floor. Please be sure to check labels for any surface warnings.

Declutter and organize the garage as much as possible. Store items stacked on shelves in an orderly fashion. If you have an excessive amount of gardening and yard tools, perhaps consider relocating them to a shed or storage unit. Your garage is included in the square footage of your home plan, and you want to maximize it's potential by keeping the space neat and tidy. Park your car in the garage.

The Yard and Perimeter

The perimeter of your yard helps 'set the container' of your home's surroundings.

If your yard is fenced it is important all railings and posts are upright and straight. If it is leaning or slacking, have the post reset.

If your yard has hedges, shrubs or trees ensure they are well manicured, trimmed and pruned. Keep your lawn maintained and weed free. If it is the dormant season, keep it free of fallen leaves.

Any items such as children's toys or bikes, garden tools, garbage cans and the like, need to be put away. The same goes for garden art, gnomes and flags. Beauty is in the eye of the beholder. Your goal is to create a clean palette, a blank slate for someone else to decorate and nest in.

If you have any trailers, old cars or accumulated debris on the property, have them removed immediately! Your yard offers a pre-emptive testimony of the pride you have for your home and how diligently you have cared for it. There is no room for untidy clutter in today's market.

If the daylight hours are shorter, please ensure the walkway to your house is clear and well lit. Inspect each individual light fixture for any wear and tear, replacing burnt out bulbs as needed and making any necessary upgrades. Solar power lights are an inexpensive and easily installed addition that can be placed along walkways. As well, they can accentuate flower beds to increase nighttime charm.

The Porch

The porch is an extension of the home's interior and as such can increase the living space. Create a welcoming atmosphere, one that subconsciously invites someone to sit and relax a moment.

Seasonal flowers in window boxes create charm and the use of colourful outdoor cushions on existing chairs is a simple way to make space inviting. While keeping the patio clear of clutter, a staged gathering area can help encourage a visitor to envision the opportunities to entertain. Many hardware stores have outdoor rugs that go above and beyond the Astroturf carpeting from yesteryear.

If your mailbox is on your porch, consider beautifying it with a fresh coat of paint. This is an easy fix that will add to your home's appeal.

The Doorway

The door is your last opportunity to emphasize curb appeal before your guest enters. Accentuate this by making the door a focal point unto itself!

Prep and paint the front door, remembering to clean, tighten and polish the door handle. Some would say that a pop of colour on the front door creates stage presence. What colors are your neighbours' front doors? Talk to your Realtor and ask for feedback.

Lay a welcome mat beneath the front door and create symmetry with a large planter box on either side of the door. Consider planting lavender, rosemary or thyme to create a lingering gentle aroma before entering. It is all about the greeting and the sensory experiences.

From The Inside Out

As buyers walk through your home, they too will be taking stock of the backyard, both through the windows as well as stepping outside before the end of the tour.

The backyard is just as important to tend to as the front! Using simple staging strategies will make the space inviting and encourage the prospective viewer to imagine how they will spend their summer weekends.

Create a casual focal point utilizing your existing patio furniture. While you want to keep the lawn clear and open to maximize the appearance of space, perhaps there is a quiet area that could be enhanced to dare the prospective buyer to daydream.

Remember to keep all children's toys out of sight, keep the lawn maintained and clean up regularly after any pets.

While keeping backyard elements simple and neutral, colorful flowers always make everything that much more welcoming. The same aromatic herbs that were suggested for next to the front door can be just as enticing on the back patio.

Often, we are spending more time outdoors, and so these outdoor areas become a natural extension of the home. This space can help maximize your house's listing price. When you are staging your front porch and or back patio, consider doing the same with any balcony, terrace or outside space. Ensure they are clean and well maintained and create a natural aesthetic.

Seasonal Curb Appeal Strategies

Houses don't just sell in the warm and sunny months. The following is a simple list of seasonal efforts that will help keep your curb appeal at its most beautiful.

Spring

- ❏ Repair any winter damage, such as painting trim, and cleaning window exteriors
- ❏ Have the gutters thoroughly cleaned
- ❏ Bring your lawn back after any winter damage, seed bald spots
- ❏ Rake wet leaves and fallen twigs
- ❏ Fertilize lawn

Summer

- ❏ Keep the lawn regularly trimmed
- ❏ Regularly rake lawn trimmings
- ❏ Pull weeds regularly
- ❏ Keep lawn watered according to local watering restrictions
- ❏ Keep plants watered
- ❏ Pay frequent attention to plants in containers and planter boxes

❑ Have chimney cleaned and inspected in time for cool autumn days

Autumn

❑ Keep leaves raked

❑ Have the gutters thoroughly cleaned

❑ Remove dead flowers and replace with autumn greenery

❑ Consider planting some simple autumn bulbs that will bloom in springtime

❑ Place a seasonal planter or pumpkin next to the doorway

❑ Fertilize lawn again if applicable

Winter

❑ Shovel your sidewalk and driveway

❑ Keep the walkway salted

❑ Remove icicles from overhead

❑ Add a ribbon or wreath to your door but resist over decorating for the holidays

❑ Keep an area to the side for visitors' wet footwear

❑ Assess and accentuate driveway lighting

Your Showcasing Ally

Do what you can ahead of time to maximize the presence of your home, and last but not least, remember to keep your window furnishings open. Not only does it look neater from the street, but it brightens the interior at the same time.

Your Realtor is a trusted ally in garnering suggestions to get your home prepared for a wow-worthy first impression. Please don't hesitate to ask your professional for suggestions and feedback and be sure to consult with them before investing any money.

About the Author, Olga Pippy

Olga believes that each family or individual is unique. As a professional full-time Real Estate Agent since 2000, she has tailored her service to meet each client's specific wants and needs. Through providing clients with the highest quality of representation, Olga has developed personal professional client relationships based on trust and support. You too can benefit from this ultimate level of customer service.

For buyers, Olga offers her "Preferred Buyers Program" based on her clients' specifications, and more importantly, Olga will keep looking for that "perfect fit", rather than have you settle for a home that isn't quite right.

For sellers, Olga offers her "Maximum Home Value" audit along with a marketing plan, which puts your listing directly in front of those buyers who are ready, willing and able to purchase.

Olga's greatest professional satisfaction is in providing her clients with a level of service guaranteed to exceed their expectations.

When it comes to selling real estate, lots of agents promise great service. Unfortunately, a promise is worthless when it is broken. That's why Olga provides you, with service guarantee in writing.

Many of the services Olga provides include:

- Endeavouring to provide you with effective, professional service.

- Communicating with you on a regular basis.

- Providing you with a Comparative Market Analysis (C.M.A.) to correctly price your home.

- Professionally present all offers and assist in the negotiation process.

- Understanding the client's wants and needs and developing a strategy to match that.

Your satisfaction is Olga's #1 priority from the initial meeting with you until you sell your home or buy your dream home.

You can reach Olga Pippy at:

Phone: 709.689.7710

Email: opippy@hotmail.com

Checklists

The following checklists were provided with permission from the Canada Mortgage and Housing Corporation.

Home Features Checklist

Is the home new or resale?	□ Resale	□ New
What kind of home is it?	□ Detached	□ Semi-detached
	□ Townhouse	□ Duplex
	□ High-rise	□ Low-rise
	□ Freehold	□ Condominium
How old is the home?	# years:	
How large is the lot?		
Is it on a quiet street?	□ Yes	□ No
What is the exterior finish?	□ Brick	□ Aluminum siding
	□ Wood	□ Vinyl siding
	□ Combination brick and siding	
What is the foundation made of?		
How many bedrooms are there?		
How many bathrooms?		
How is the home heated?	□ Gas	□ Oil

	□ Electric	□ Wood
Does it have air conditioning?	□ Central	□ Window
Does the master bedroom have its own bathroom?	□ Yes	□ No
Is there a bath-room on the ground floor?	□ Yes	□ No
Is there an eat-in kitchen?	□ Yes	□ No
A separate dining room?	□ Yes	□ No
A separate family room?	□ Yes	□ No
A fireplace or woodstove?	□ Yes	□ No
A spare room for an office?	□ Yes	□ No
Does the base-ment have enough space for storage or a workshop?	□ Yes	□ No
Is there a deck or patio?	□ Yes	□ No
A private drive-way?	□ Yes	□ No
Garage or carport?	□ Garage	□ Carport

Does the home have a security system?	□ Yes	□ No
Is the home accessible (for seniors or people with a disability)?	□ Yes	□ No
How close is the home (in kms) to:	Your work	Your spouse's work
	Public transportation	Schools
	Shopping	Parks/playgrounds
	Recreational facilities	Restaurants
	Place of worship	Veterinarian
	Police station	Fire station
	Hospital	Doctor/dentist

Home Hunting Comparison Worksheet

HOME #1	HOME #2	HOME #3
Real estate rep: Tel:	Real estate rep: Tel:	Real estate rep: Tel:
Type of home: Sq. ft.:	Type of home: Sq. ft.:	Type of home: Sq. ft.:
# bedrooms:	# bedrooms:	# bedrooms:
Year built:	Year built:	Year built:
Occupancy date:	Occupancy date:	Occupancy date:
Asking price: $	Asking price: $	Asking price: $
Annual Costs	***Annual Costs***	***Annual Costs***
Property taxes $	Property taxes $	Property taxes $
Utilities $	Utilities $	Utilities $
Insurance $	Insurance $	Insurance $
Condo fees $	Condo fees $	Condo fees $
Other $	Other $	Other $
TOTAL $	TOTAL $	TOTAL $
Neighbourhood	***Neighbourhood***	***Neighbourhood***
Distance to work:	Distance to work:	Distance to work:
To spouse's work:	To spouse's work:	To spouse's work:
To schools:	To schools:	To schools:
To shopping:	To shopping:	To shopping:
To playgrounds:	To playgrounds:	To playgrounds:
To hospital:	To hospital:	To hospital:

To police station:	To police station:	To police station:
To fire station:	To fire station:	To fire station:
To place of worship:	To place of worship:	To place of worship:
Other notes:	*Other notes:*	*Other notes:*

Monthly Homeowner Budget

Monthly Budget	
Housing Expenses	**Average Cost Each Month**
Mortgage payment (principal and interest)	$
Electricity	$
Heating costs	$
Maintenance and repairs	$
Parking (if paid separately)	$
Property insurance	$
Property taxes	$
Water	$
Other Expenses	
Cable TV/Satellite/Video rental	$
Car fuel	$
Car insurance and license	$
Car repairs and service	$
Charitable donations	$
Child care (if applicable	$
Child support/Alimony (if applicable)	$
Clothing	$
Dental expenses	$
Entertainment and recreation	$
Groceries/food	$
Home furnishings	$
Internet	$
Life and property insurance	$
Medical expenses, prescriptions, eyewear	$
Newspapers, magazines, books	$
Personal items	$
Public transportation	$
Restaurants	$
Savings	$
Telephone/Cell phone	$
Other expenses	$
Total Monthly Expenses	$

CHECKLIST: Planning Your Move

2 to 3 weeks before you move:

□ Buy boxes and other moving supplies □ Donate or throw away unwanted items □ Take toxic household cleaners, old paint and other chemicals to your local Toxic Waste Centre	□ Contact Canada Post to forward your mail to your new address □ Arrange for telephone service at your new home □ Arrange to return any Cable TV equipment to your cable company
□ Make any necessary travel arrangements or reservations	□ Transfer your car insurance and license plates if needed
□ Notify your children's old school and register at their new school	□ Get copies of all medical, dental and veterinary records
Contact or send change of address cards to: □ Driver's license, Health cards, Insurance	□ Employer(s), doctor, dentist
□ Magazines and other subscriptions	□ Memberships
□ Canada Customs and Revenue Agency	□ Bank accounts and credit cards

1 to 2 weeks before you move:

□ Return anything you have borrowed	□ Safely dispose of any flammable materials
□ Arrange for your major appliances to be moved (if you will be taking them with you)	□ Arrange to disconnect utilities at your old home and connect utilities at your new home

2 to 7 days before you move:

□ Find out what you can bring with you if you are	□ Pack a suitcase or small box with the clothes and

traveling by car, bus, train or plane	other things you will need for the first few days in your new home
The day before you move:	
□ Take down your curtains and curtain rods	□ Pack all of your personal items except for anything you will need tonight and tomorrow
□ Empty and defrost the refrigerator and clean the stove	□ Collect all your keys and keep them in a safe place
Moving day:	
□ Keep your paperwork where you can find it	□ Clean your old home or apartment and inspect it with the landlord
□ Pack all your bedding linens, toiletries, etc □ Do a final "walk through" to check every room, closet and cabinet to be sure you aren't forgetting anything □ If you hired a moving company, walk through your home with the supervisor to make a list of all your boxes and belongings	□ Confirm your new address with the moving company, and ask what time they will be arriving □ Make sure you know how to contact your new landlord or superintendent

Glossary

Amortization: The length of time required to completely pay off a mortgage, if all payments are made on time.

Appraisal: An estimate of the current market value of a property.

Appraiser: A professional who determines the market value of a property or home.

Blended Payment: A mortgage payment that includes both the principal loan amount and the interest in one payment. The payment amount stays the same throughout, but the percentage of the payment that go towards the principal or interest change as time progresses.

Closed Mortgage: This type of mortgage cannot be prepaid or renegotiated before the end of the term without the lender's permission and a financial penalty.

Closing Costs: The costs a buyer must pay in addition to the purchase price of a home or property. These include legal fees, transfer fees and disbursements. Closing costs generally range from 1.5% to 4% of the purchase price.

Closing Date: The date at which the sale of a property becomes final and the new owner makes a final walk through and takes possession of the home.

Conditional Offer: An Offer to Purchase a home that is subject to conditions that must be met before the sale is final (for example, arranging financing or a home inspection).

Conventional Mortgage: A mortgage loan for up to 80% of the value of a property.

Counteroffer: If a buyer's offer to the seller is not accepted as-is, the seller may counter the offer by changing something, such as the closing date or price.

Credit Report: The report from the credit bureau that determines how good or bad your credit is.

Deed: A legal document signed by both the buyer and seller to transfer ownership of a home.

Default: Failing to abide by the terms of an agreement. If you miss paying your mortgage payments, your lender can foreclose on your home.

Delinquency: Failing to make a payment on time.

Deposit: Money placed in trust by a home buyer when he or she makes an Offer to Purchase a home. The deposit is held by a third party (i.e. the real estate brokerage or lawyer) until the sale is complete.

Down Payment: The amount of money not covered by the mortgage, and which you must pay out of your own savings.

Home inspector: A professional who inspects every aspect of a home to determine if anything needs to be repaired or replaced.

Maturity Date: When the term of the mortgage ends. On this day, the mortgage loan must be renewed or paid in full.

MLS (Multiple Listing Service): A service offered by real estate boards with listings of the homes that are currently for sale.

Mortgage: A loan to buy a house or property, usually paid monthly or bi-monthly with regular payments.

Offer to Purchase: An offer in writing that specifies the terms under which a buyer agrees to buy a home or property and which is presented to the seller. If the offer is accepted by the seller, it becomes a legally binding contract.

Open Mortgage: A mortgage that can be paid off or renegotiated at any time without any penalty.

Principal: The amount of money that you borrow for a loan or mortgage.

Property Insurance: Insurance that protects your home and your belongings in case your home or building is damaged or destroyed.

Property Taxes: Taxes charged annually by the municipality.